MW01148495

Hippopotamus

by Grace Hansen

Abdo
AFRICAN ANIMALS
Kids

abdopublishing.com

Published by Abdo Kids, a division of ABDO, P.O. Box 398166, Minneapolis, Minnesota 55439.

Copyright © 2018 by Abdo Consulting Group, Inc. International copyrights reserved in all countries. No part of this book may be reproduced in any form without written permission from the publisher.

Printed in the United States of America, North Mankato, Minnesota.

102017

012018

 THIS BOOK CONTAINS RECYCLED MATERIALS

Photo Credits: iStock, Minden Pictures, Shutterstock

Production Contributors: Teddy Borth, Jennie Forsberg, Grace Hansen

Design Contributors: Dorothy Toth, Laura Mitchell

Publisher's Cataloging in Publication Data

Names: Hansen, Grace, author.

Title: Hippopotamus / by Grace Hansen.

Description: Minneapolis, Minnesota : Abdo Kids, 2018. | Series: African animals |
          Includes glossary, index and online resource (page 24).

Identifiers: LCCN 2017943135 | ISBN 9781532104183 (lib.bdg.) | ISBN 9781532105302 (ebook) |
          ISBN 9781532105869 (Read-to-me ebook)

Subjects: LCSH: Hippopotamuses--Juvenile literature. | Zoology--Africa--Juvenile literature.

Classification: DDC 599.63 --dc23

LC record available at https://lccn.loc.gov/2017943135

Table of Contents

Hippo Habitats

Hippopotamuses live in Africa. They are often found near bodies of water.

4

They spend most of their days in water. The African sun can be very hot. Hippos need to stay cool.

Food

At night, hippos leave the water. They walk up to 5 miles (8 km) to find grass and fruit to eat. They are often back in the water by sunrise.

9

Body

A hippo's **nostrils**, eyes, and
ears sit on top of its head.
It can be almost completely
underwater. But it can still
breathe, see, and hear.

10

Hippos have very large, barrel-shaped bodies. They weigh between 5,000 and 8,000 pounds (2,268 to 3,629 kg)!

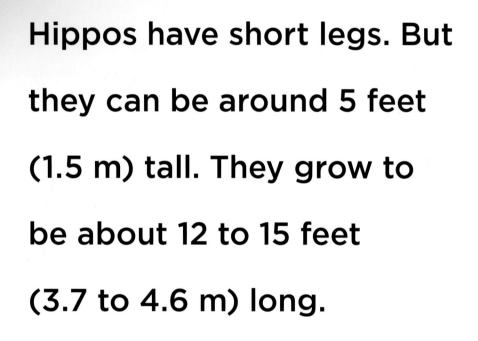

Hippos have short legs. But they can be around 5 feet (1.5 m) tall. They grow to be about 12 to 15 feet (3.7 to 4.6 m) long.

Hippos have very big mouths.

If a hippo opens its mouth, it

can be 4 to 5 feet (1.2 to 1.5 m)

from top to bottom!

Groups

Hippos live in small groups. The group is led by one large male. Females, smaller adult males, and baby hippos are also in the group.

19

Baby Hippos

Females have one baby hippo at a time. A baby hippo weighs around 100 pounds (45.4 kg) at birth. It drinks its mother's milk for about 18 months.

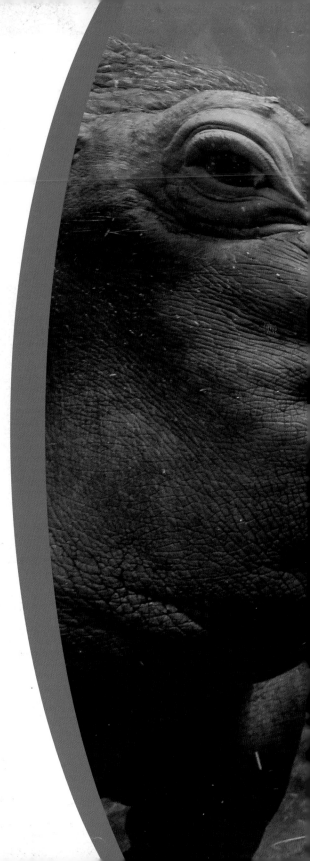

More Facts

- The word "hippopotamus" comes from the Greek language. The Greek words **translate** to "water horse," because of a hippo's size and the time it spends in the water.

- The male leader protects his area and group by fighting other males. Males fight each other with their large teeth and **tusks**.

- Hippos need to eat a lot. A hippo can eat around 80 pounds (36.3 kg) of grass in one night!

Glossary

nostril – one of the two openings of the nose that allows for breathing.

translate – to turn from one language into another.

tusk – a long, large, pointed tooth that sticks out from the mouth of some animals.

Index

Abdo Kids ONLINE

FREE! ONLINE MULTIMEDIA RESOURCES

Visit **abdokids.com** and use this code to access crafts, games, videos, and more!

Abdo Kids Code:
AHK4183